DAVID W. PREUS

AUGSBURG PUBLISHING HOUSE
MINNEAPOLIS, MINNESOTA

GO WITH THE GOSPEL

Copyright © 1977 Augsburg Publishing House

Library of Congress Catalog Card No. 76-27075

International Standard Book No. 0-8066-1560-5

All rights reserved. No part of this book may be used or reproduced in any manner whatsoever without written permission except in the case of brief quotations embodied in critical articles and reviews. For information address Augsburg Publishing House, 426 South Fifth Street, Minneapolis, Minnesota 55415.

Scripture quotations unless otherwise noted are from the Revised Standard Version of the Bible, copyright 1946, 1952, and 1971 by the Division of Christian Education of the National Council of Churches.

MANUFACTURED IN THE UNITED STATES OF AMERICA

Contents

A Word to the Reader 5

PART ONE:

Sermons on the Great Commission

Who Is in Charge? 9
Go with the Gospel 16
Go—Make Disciples 24
Go—to All Nations 32
Go—Baptize 40
Go—Teaching Them to Observe 49
Go—I Am with You Always 59
Go—to the Close of the Age 68

PART TWO:

Reflections on Evangelical Outreach

What Is Evangelical Outreach? 79
Lutheran Identity and Witness 85
A Time to Reach Out 93
Lutheran Evangelical Outreach 102

A Word to the Reader

American Lutherans need to renew emphasis on evangelical outreach. Conventions and councils in both The American Lutheran Church and the Lutheran Church in America have recognized that fact. As a result the two church bodies have called their congregations to respond anew to Christ's charge to "go, make disciples."

The Great Commission in Matthew 20:18-20 is a constant reminder of God's intent to share his life with all people. God has chosen the Gospel witness of his followers as the primary vehicle for accomplishing his intent.

Publishing a series of sermons on the Great Commission has two primary purposes. First, the sermons summon *all* congregation members to participate actively in evangelical outreach. Witness to Christ needs to be made in normal everyday occurrences. Evangelical outreach is not the responsibility of the clergy alone.

Second, the use of sermons indicates the importance of preaching in a Lutheran emphasis on evangelical outreach. We believe in the power of God present in the preached word. It is important, therefore, that Christ's charge to "go, make disciples" be heard from the pulpits of Lutheran congregations. There can be no major emphasis in Lutheran congregations unless the emphasis is grounded in God's word and proclaimed from the pulpit. Hopefully, these sermons will encourage pastors to preach on Matthew 20:18-20.

The thoughts in the second part of the book are reflections on the nature of an evangelical outreach emphasis and why such an emphasis is especially important for Lutherans at this time. These four chapters might well serve as the basis for study and discussion in adult classes.

It is my strong conviction that God's word calls Lutheran people, together with all Christian people, to a strengthened Gospel outreach. Christ's command is clear. The need is apparent. He has supplied us with the Gospel and great human resources. It is up to us to use them.

DAVID W. PREUS

Part One

SERMONS

on the

Great Commission

Who Is in Charge?

And Jesus came and said to them, "All authority in heaven and on earth has been given to me. Go therefore . . ." (Matthew 28:18-19)

The question of authority is a big question indeed. Who is in charge of existence? How did we come to be here? What is expected of us? Is there a trustworthy, authoritative word from someone in charge? From whom shall I take my orders for living? Or are we tossed into this earthly existence simply to fend for ourselves for a few years, to make of existence what we will?

There are always people about who claim authority. Human history is littered with tyrants who claimed the authority to rule over others. Nations have repeatedly claimed some kind of divine right that justifies the subjugation and exploitation of people. "Company towns" describes communities in which the people are virtually owned by the company. Humans have practiced slavery, the ultimate in claiming authority over the lives of others. In the face of all these claims of authority the question remains . . . Who is in charge?

Christ as Authority

The Christian church has had that question answered in this word from our Lord Jesus Christ. "All authority has been given me." God, who created all that is and sustains it with his continuing creative power, exercises his authority through the person of his son, Jesus Christ. We acknowledge that authority when we call him "Lord" and take up citizenship in his kingdom. But how do we get to that point? What possibly can bring us to say, "Yes, I believe that Jesus is Lord, the supreme power and authority in all created existence, and especially in my life"?

The ultimate answer to the question of how one comes to believe in the authoritative lordship of Jesus is stated clearly in Luther's small catechism. "I believe that I cannot by my own reason or strength believe in Jesus Christ my Lord or come to him, but the Holy Spirit has called me through the Gospel." It is the Spirit of God himself who convinces us, through the good news about Jesus Christ.

A Servant Authority

God has exercised his sovereign power and authority, not by setting up an earthly kingdom with coercive military might or economic domination, not by overwhelming us in the court of human logic, but by sending his son to be the loving, saving servant of all humanity. We are convinced of his authority, not by his awesome displays of raw power, but by his person, his words and his works. It is in taking the form of a servant that God exercises his authority among us. It is the convincing reality of the person of Jesus that brings us to recognition of his authority. There is a strange drawing power in the central Gospel story of Jesus taking the cross, wrestling it out to a hill, suffering and dying on it, and then three days later being raised from the dead. When we confess that Jesus is Lord, it is not because we have decided it is so but because he has convinced us it is so.

There is no self-serving in the life and work of Jesus. He does not manipulate us or use us for his own ends. He saves us for our sakes, not his.

He does not need us, but we need him. His authority is established on the basis of his suffering love, not on the basis of brute power. He uses his authority to forgive sins rather than require sacrifices. In coming to faith and submitting to his lordship, we find ourselves not enslaved, but set free. That is why it becomes sheer delight to acknowledge his authority. You know he will call forth the best in you, not the worst. You know he calls you to be loved and to love, not to become predatory and proud. You discover his forgiving love is patient and kind, restoring you again and again. You believe God wants you as his child and heir, not as an unwilling slave. You find yourself at home in the universe, becoming the person you know you are meant to be.

It is because of these things that the church tirelessly tells the story of God's mighty acts of love. God has shown his power and authority in raising Jesus from the dead and establishing his lordship over all things. He has made it possible for us to live with confidence amidst the ambiguities and uncertainties and tragedies of earthly existence. Through Christ's resurrection he has shown us the final scene and assured its goodness. The Easter victory makes possible a discipleship that is not dependent on earthly ease or well-being.

Scripture as Authority

Until such time as life on this earth ends, the living Word, Christ, exercises his authority through the written word, the Scriptures. One of the cardinal objectives of the Reformation was to reestablish the authority of the Scriptures over the church. The church of the Reformation continues to picture itself as an obedient subject to the Scriptures. The church's authority, therefore, is always Christ as he speaks through the Scriptures. All of our words, all of the church's decisions and confessions are subject to the corrective word of the Scriptures. We are to "test the spirits" by submitting all claims to the authority of Scripture.

The Scriptures are the means by which God makes known his sovereign will for his people. They are God's assurance that the good news about Christ will not be lost or distorted. Thus it is that the church gathers regularly to hear the Scriptures read and to hear sermons preached on the biblical texts. For this reason Bible study is encouraged as a life-time activity. The telling and retelling of the biblical stories has always been an essential part of the nurture of the entire Christian family, both children and adults. And also the memorization of key biblical texts has always been an important element in a Christian's devotional life.

There is always a temptation for the church to use the Bible as a legalistic rule book rather than as the means by which Christ himself comes to his people. When that happens, the Bible becomes wooden and impersonal. The church turns to endless debate about the Bible rather than obedience to the Bible. The Bible is not to be venerated. It is to be used. It is not enough to insist that God is in charge, we are to discover what he charges us to do. So in the Matthew 28:18-20 text that is the subject for these sermons, we discover not only that all authority has been given to Christ, but that his authoritative word to us is "Go, make disciples." In responding to that word of command we bear witness to our faith in the authority of Christ and his word.

The Church's Authority

The church is able to speak with authority not because it is inherently holy, but because it speaks the word it has been given. When the pastor declares the forgiveness of sins to penitent, believing sinners, it is by the authority of Christ, attested in the Scriptures that forgiveness is given. The authority is not in the pastor, but in the word he speaks. When Christians confess the Apostles', Nicene, or Athanasian Creeds as authoritative, they do so in the conviction that they are true summary statements of what God has done for us and said to us as recorded in the Scriptures. When the congregation gathers to worship, it does so not to meet a need for group therapy but in the conviction that God has called his people together to worship him and to receive his blessing. When the church exhorts its people to go out and make disciples, it does so not to assure its institutional survival but because God has given the order to "go make disciples." The church speaks authoritatively as it tells of God's mighty acts, as it speaks God's word and not the word of its own devising.

Who Is in Charge?

Who is in charge? Is there a trustworthy, authoritative word from someone who is in charge? From whom shall I take my orders for living? Hear the word of God from the mouth of Jesus, "All authority has been given unto me in heaven and on earth." You are invited to join the whole Christian church on earth and all the heavenly host in declaring from your heart that God is in charge, that he exercises his authority through Jesus Christ his son, and that it is from him you take your orders for living.

Amen.

Go with the Gospel

Go . . . (Matthew 28:19)

"Go! Go! Go! Go!" is the drumming, penetrating cry that beats with passion in the heat of a closely fought game. If you have played in such a game, you know how the adrenalin starts flowing. It may spur you on to your finest performance.

Something similar happens when followers of Christ encounter the Great Commission. God says go! Go with the Gospel! He sends you as messengers bringing word of great victory. You are his good will ambassador to people of all nations who have not known of his kingdom. You are his witnesses, telling of his creative power, his hatred of evil, and his great love for his people.

Go with the Gospel

You are his town criers, shouting out the good news of God's salvation through Jesus Christ.

You are not called to be speculators in a spiritual stock market inviting people to take their choice. Neither are you scientists who attempt to convince the world's doubters that you have proved what they doubt. No! you are God's messengers to a sin-bound humanity declaring that God has redeemed his people through Jesus Christ. You are asked to declare the triumph of Christ over all the principalities and powers that twist and destroy people. Whether homemaker, analyst, professor, or farmer, you are asked to carry God's Gospel to others.

Witnessing Christians

The Christian church is always at its best when its people are excited about going with the Gospel. After Jesus' death his followers were quiet and depressed. They were in hiding. Suddenly women disciples broke into their recesses with the news that the tomb had been burst. "He is risen," they cried. "Christ lives!" They did not keep the good news to themselves. They carried the message to their friends. What a change that effected. Suddenly there was movement, excitement, and a new sense of purpose.

When the rest of the disciples were convinced that Christ had indeed risen from the dead, they, too, were ready to go with the Gospel. Peter, who a few days before had three times fearfully denied knowing Jesus, was suddenly risking his life preaching the good news from the steps of the temple. The threats of the authorities, the odds against success, the ridicule of neighbors, just did not matter. Those early disciples heard the Lord's charge to "go with the Gospel" and they went. They set the tone of the Christian church's perennial response to Christ's command, "You shall be my witnesses in Jerusalem, and in all Judea, and Samaria, and to the end of the earth" (Acts 1:8).

Again and again in the years since, the church has recaptured its sense of excitement and enthusiasm by responding anew to Christ's charge to go with the Gospel. It has seldom been easy going. Others have shared the experience of the Apostle Paul in being imprisoned, beaten, reviled, and ridiculed for the Gospel's sake. Many of Christ's witnesses have been met by a wall of unbelief, disinterest, and boredom. Nevertheless, through the persistent witness and persevering love of his witnesses, Christ has made himself known to an ever-broadening band of believers.

Lutheran Witnesses

The time is at hand for a resurgent witnessing spirit among American Lutherans. Listen anew to God's word that sends us going with the Gospel. Many of you are steady supporters of missionary efforts and regular participants in public worship and private prayer. Some of you have also found personal ways to carry the Gospel. God bless you for that. You have been an inspiration to all of us. In general, however, American Lutherans have had a parochial attitude. We have tended to gather in ethnic congregational groupings. There has been a reluctance to share the fellowship, not really believing that others were ready to share our faith. That was understandable and perhaps necessary during the immigrant years. For most of us, however, the immigrant years are past. Lutheran congregations are already ethnically mixed. It has been amply demonstrated that when Lutherans are outgoing evangelists, American people from all walks of life are ready to share their faith and life. God has commissioned his Lutheran Christians, together with all Christians, to go with the Gospel. Only our faint-heartedness prevents this from being one of the great moments in Lutheran history.

A Christian congregation is not meant to gather for periodic hand-wringing exercises as its membership dwindles or its strength is eroded. Neither need a congregation think it must be large in numbers before it can be a vigorous and attractive body of Christ's people. If that were so, the church would never have gotten beyond Jerusalem. New beginnings are always the result of some small group of people being convinced it is time to be on the move regardless of the difficulties. Within a congregation the call to renewed vigorous witness is often heard first by some small group within that congregation. They join each other in prayer, encourage each other in witness, support each other in seeming failure, and rejoice with each other over each life claimed by the Spirit of God.

You and the Gospel

Today God asks *you* to go with the Gospel. He asks you to tell the old, old story of Jesus and his love. He asks you to tell the story whenever and wherever you can. You do not need to be clever, wise, or powerful. You need recognize only that God has claimed you through the story of Jesus and that he will do the same with others.

You are asked to find your way as his witness. You are asked to find others in your congregation who will join you in prayer, in planning, and in reaching out to others. You are to be the means by which God draws others into his believing family. It is a heady charge. You can find many ways to be busy with many other things. Do not be sidetracked. God will see that your life counts. You will find excitement and fulfillment as his witness.

Hang in There

As a member of a church fellowship you are asked to pool your resources with other members and send out special missionaries. You may be the one called to go in that capacity, or you may be among those who support such a one with prayers and money and encouragement. That is the way the Gospel has been made known to our ancestors and to us. That is the way the good news continues to be carried today to people throughout the world.

Even as you are encouraged to be one who goes with the Gospel, it must be said that it is not the only word God speaks to his people. Sometimes we have to hear God say, "Hang on, I am with you," or "Comfort ye, comfort ye, my people." That was true for generations of Japanese Christians who had to live under the threat of death if they were discovered. That was true for a brave German Christian who served as a hated SS officer in World War II in order to get solid data on what was taking place in concentration camps. It was true for the reformer, John Huss, as he stood at the stake where he was to be burned for being a heretic. It is true for many whose physical impairments keep them confined and often alone. Even in such circumstances, however, people find opportunity to go with the Gospel. Christ's witnesses always need to be undergirded by supportive prayer. Many a sickroom has become a sanctuary as a bedfast disciple has maintained a ministry of prayer. Others have used an endless stream of letters as vehicles of witness. Paul and Silas turned their imprisonment into a hymn sing and the result was the baptism of a jailer and his family. Pastor Dietrich Bonhoeffer, on the day of his execution in a Nazi prison, spent his last hours bringing the Gospel and the sacraments to those imprisoned with him.

God's good news about Christ has a way of finding ever new outlets. Grace does not stay fixed in position nor does it operate by static rules. God's love, Christ's leadership, and the ingenuity of people make for endless new possibilities. You are asked to give your best and bravest efforts to effective witness. God promises to stand by you.

The Cheering Crowd

As you go with the Gospel, you are to know also that you are cheered on by all those who

Go with the Gospel

have witnessed to Christ in all times and places. The opening verses of Hebrews 12 remind us of that. "Therefore, since we are surrounded by so great a cloud of witnesses, let us also lay aside every weight, and sin which clings so closely, and let us run with perseverance the race that is set before us, looking to Jesus the pioneer and perfecter of our faith."

Our Lord Jesus charges you to go with the Gospel. With faith's eyes and ears you can then see and hear that whole stadium full of your fellow witnesses, those who have gone on before you, echoing Christ's word at the top of their voices, "Go, go, go, go!" Whatever your fears, whatever your limitations, whatever your doubts, whatever the hardships, the word is go. Go with the Gospel! In Jesus' name, go!

Amen.

Go—
Make Disciples

Go therefore and make disciples.
(Matthew 28:19)

Faith in Jesus Christ is an intensely private concern. Nobody can have faith for you. It is a matter between God and you. Faith in Christ, however, never remains a private affair. As soon as he has a hold on us, he urges us to enlist others. Go into the highways and byways and invite all to the wedding feast; proclaim the good news; gather the flock; preach the Gospel in season and out; be my witnesses. The closer the walk with Christ, the more one hears the charge to "Go, make disciples."

That does not allow for coercion, however. We are to persuade, but not force. We are to befriend, but not bribe. Christians have not always been clear on that. Some generations have used the sword to require baptism. Our generation is tempted to use a subtler form of coercion called manipulation. We have techniques learned from 20th century advertisers. Christ's people are to forswear any form of coercion. But respect for another's freedom must never diminish Christian concern for getting the message across. We are to share our Lord's concern that all shall be "saved and come to the knowledge of the truth." Faithful discipleship means that we zealously, openly, avowedly seek to make disciples. We are called to be, without apology, a missionary people.

Early Witnesses

It is easy to feel inadequate to the task. Think of how those first disciples must have felt. They were a handful. They had already failed the Lord on more than one occasion. They were not in any way superior to those to whom they were sent. They were not in positions of power. They could not make disciples by superior intellect or superior logic. Yet they were charged to make disciples of all nations. How simple it would have been for them to be intimidated by such a charge.

Those early disciples had seen the resurrected Lord, however. It was to him they bore witness.

They testified to his mighty deeds and his power-filled words. They taught what he taught them. They shared what he shared with them. They quit worrying about their faith, their strengths, and their attractiveness. They told about God, about his faithfulness, his love, his power, and his fellowship. They preached Christ crucified, a stumbling block to the Jews and an offense to the Greeks. They depended on the spirit of God to do the convincing. His word, his promise to be present, gave them courage to fan out in many directions seeking to make disciples. They encountered opposition, ridicule, even persecution, and martyrdom. Only death silenced them. Even then their witnessing words and deeds lived after them. God was at work in their preaching and teaching and writing and doing. In nation after nation the church was given birth and grew.

Today's Witnesses

If we were sent out to declare our superiority over other humans we would be right to be intimidated. That is not the message, however. We are not sent out to proclaim anything about ourselves. The message is God, living, powerful, and active in history, rescuing his people through the redeeming work of Jesus Christ. It is as disciples proclaim the good news of God's love, it is as disciples zealously seek to share that love, that other disciples are made.

You believers, you who have come to faith in Christ, you are God's chosen vehicles for his word to others in this day. You are the ones who can hold Jesus before others today. You can recount his words and deeds in ways that speak to people now. You can share your faith and awe at Bethlehem's birth and Calvary's death. You can find ways to declare that Jesus is Lord today, risen from the dead to rule forever. Each of you has an audience. Family, friends, neighbors, all are people who, like you, need God. You must show them that you care whether they know the love of Christ. It is not enough to hope they will become disciples. Go—ask, encourage, exhort, persuade. Some of those people will discover that God is indeed out looking for them, through you.

Invitation to Life With God

There are three invitations you should offer as you seek to make disciples. The first has already been indicated. You invite people to share the Christian faith, to share the person, power, and love of Christ. There are many ways in which this invitation to faith may be made. One to one personal witness, public preaching, Bible studies, and quiet dialog may all be used effectively. It is your task to create the opportunities for people to hear the invitation to faith from the words of Jesus himself. "Come to me . . . trust me . . . abide in me . . . I have come that you might have life . . ." Those words carry their own dynamic, their own power.

People need to hear you say that God is the center of life, life in general and your own life. You talk to your peers about your family, your work, your trips, your garden. You talk about anything that interests you. You are asked also to talk about God. Tell how the Scriptures witness to God's dealings with his people. Talk about the faith and strength and encouragement God gives. Talk about the people of God and their life with God from Abraham's day to today.

You need not be judgmental in bearing witness to God. After all, you are not the judge. Neither need you be ashamed of talking about the love of God. It is always a compliment for a person to share what is at the heart of his or her life. Christ's people are meant to be winsome, but winsome in being bold witnesses to the crucified and risen Lord Jesus Christ. You need not be a nuisance or a nut in the manner of your invitation to faith. You make introductions all the time. You find ways to do it appropriately, without embarrassment. In the same manner you are called to introduce people to God.

Invitation to Church

The second invitation is to share the fellowship. "Come to church with us." Never minimize the witness of a congregation gathered to worship the Triune God, present in Word and sacrament. When worship is active and not passive, when preaching points to the living God of authority and power, when personal faith and friendship reach out from the congregation and surround a person, when a sense of mission pervades the assembly, people's lives will be touched by the Spirit of God.

All kinds of human needs are met by a vital Christian congregation. Loneliness is met by friendship. Alienation is met by acceptance. Guilt is met by forgiveness. Despair is met by hope. Meaninglessness is met by mission. Doubt is met by faith. Insecurity is met by assurance. We are made to belong. At its deepest level that need to belong is met by the church in a way that cannot be matched by clan, club, or country. We belong to God and to God's family. Every other level of community is transitory, bound to this earth. The communion of saints alone binds us together in the eternal family.

Be bold in inviting others into the life and worship of the congregation. The Word and sacraments will always assure the presence of

God. The fellowship of sinners who live in daily forgiveness will bring needed encouragement. Hymns of faith and fellowship in prayer will exercise faith's muscles and help people be strong.

Invitation to Mission

The third invitation is to be partners in mission. Discipleship is more than faith in God, more than fellowship in the church. It also involves participation in mission. Jesus said, "Follow me." He also said, "If you continue in my word then are you my disciples indeed." His intention is not only to rescue people from sin, death, and despair, but also to make us over into new creatures. We are called to "die to ourselves in order to live unto God."

Do not hesitate in inviting others to give themselves to God in obedient discipleship. People need to find meaning for their lives. Self-gratification is not a sufficient mission to keep people healthy. Be bold in using Christ's call to partnership in mission.

You cannot dictate the nature of another person's fulfillment in mission. Every Christian is asked to find his or her own individual ways to serve. Each is to use whatever gifts God has bestowed. You can, however, help new Christians understand and share in the corporate mission of the church. You can encourage them to personally share in the witnessing work of the church and also to share in the support of the world-wide missionary work of the church. You can encourage them to be merciful in their individual lives and also support the institutions of mercy that the church maintains. You can encourage church members to stand with the poor and oppressed, to join with all persons of good will in creating townships, cities, states, and nations that are communities of dignity and decency, "with liberty and justice for all."

People are attracted to congregations that are centers for mission. We are attracted to individuals who have found a cause larger than themselves. All of us instinctively know that God has not called his people to maintain the status quo. You are the very people who can make your congregation a great center for God's mission on earth. By your faith active in love you can glorify God and create an inviting congregation.

Our Lord is always looking for disciples. He has arranged for you to go with the invitation to discipleship. His invitation is extended to all. Go, in every way you can find, and make his invitation known. His word to you is clear . . . "Go, make disciples!"

Amen.

Go—
to All Nations

Go, therefore, and make disciples of all nations.
(Matthew 28:19)

That word remains staggering in its audacity. It was first addressed to a handful of fishermen and farmers, homemakers and shopkeepers, who lived in one of many minor satellite provinces of the Roman Empire. They were told to make disciples of people of different religions, languages, loyalties, customs, mores, and colors. Never mind how different they are or how far away they live. Go, make disciples of them all.

The charge has not changed. It comes across the centuries to us who are Christ's followers today. Be concerned about your witness to family and friends and neighbors, of course. Begin your missionary work right where you are. But never stop there. You are charged to be party to an "all nations" effort. God's saving word is for all. You are a part of God's strategy for making disciples of all nations.

A Personal Faith

Life with God is intensely personal. Everyone who is captured by the grace of God knows of that private inner life with God. Our devotional life reflects this intensely personal character. Certainly the popularity of the 23rd Psalm indicates the depth of personal faith. "The Lord is *my* shepherd . . ." Our hymnody gives similar utterance again and again.

> *Yet I may love thee too, O Lord,*
> *Almighty as thou art*
> *For thou hast stooped to ask of me*
> *The love of my poor heart.*

Who can but be moved by Jesus' assurance that "not a sparrow falls to the ground . . . even the hairs of your head are all numbered." Nothing about you is outside the concern of our heavenly father. Christian faith is personal and private and it calls forth a personal and private response.

A Missionary Faith

Life with God is never just personal, however. God does not call you only to a private tryst with him. Neither does he join you only to a local family of believers. It is a temptation for us to think it so. How often a congregational meeting hears a member declare that "we need it here" when someone suggests that more money should be spent in the world mission of the church. "Take care of everything at home first" is the cry. Then if anything is left over we can think about others.

Most of us would not have heard the Gospel yet today if Christ's disciples had heeded such voices. The church would have had a hard time getting out of Jerusalem if the apostles had given absolute priority to the local ministry. The church has often become stuffy and parochial, weak and inactive, a defender of the status quo, when it has not heard and heeded God's missionary mandate to all nations. Yes, God means for us to have a local concern for making disciples. He simultaneously calls us to a global concern. "Go make disciples of all nations" is his word. That means that nation in which you hold citizenship plus every other nation in the world.

The Christian church has manifested a world missionary concern throughout its history. The record of the missionary journeys of Paul, as recorded in the book of Acts and witnessed in his epistles, has become an important part of Christian Scripture. Already in apostolic days we read of the church spreading out of Asia Minor into Africa and Europe and India. New centers of Christian faith in turn became sending centers for more missionaries. Traders carried the Gospel along with their wares and the church grew on many fronts.

Lutheran Christians have sought to be faithful in response to our Lord's missionary charge. The membership of the Lutheran World Federation gives testimony to the breadth of that effort. The LWF includes 95 Lutheran Churches from 51 different countries around the world. All of them are the result of missionary activity and all of them continue to have missionary activity as a fundamental charge. The lesson is obvious. Where faithful witness to the Lord Jesus Christ is made, God is faithful to give birth to faith in the hearts of others.

The story of Christian missions has not been one success story after another, however. There have been failures. There have been blunders. There have been frequent indications of a lack of missionary concern. The fact is that the population of the world is expanding at a rate considerably in excess of the rate of Christian growth. The percentage of Christians in the world is lower than it was some years ago. There is no reason for Christians to be triumphal about Christian gains. Yet, there is reason to trust the transforming power of the Gospel. God's charge was not given lightly and it is not to be taken lightly. He has declared his intent that we be his instruments in bringing all nations to discipleship. There is no alternative for us but to fulfill that charge with enthusiasm.

Evangelical Outreach

That means that our churches must carry a high priority for evangelical outreach at home and abroad. It means regular and fervent prayer for missions in the congregations of the church. It means encouraging young people to devote their lives to the missionary task. It means equipping the traders of this day with training and encouragement for a lay witness in far places. It means regular gifts of money to support the work that is established and the people whom the church sends. It means bringing together mission boards to study the world scene and determine where our churches can best concentrate their efforts. It means joining ecumenical agencies so Christian denominations steward their missionary resources wisely.

It means language schools, cultural studies, and Bible translating. In order that we show Christ's concern for the whole person, it frequently also means educational services, health services, and agricultural services. The whole missionary enterprise is not a cultural imperialism, but an attempt to show, by word and deed, the father's love for his earthly children.

Bridging the Boundaries

Through missionary work Christian people are constantly at work to keep boundaries from becoming hostile barriers. Familial, tribal, national, and racial boundaries have always been a part of the human scene. Frequently those boundaries have been crossed only for purposes of destruction and pillage. Christians seek to cross them as sisters and brothers in the faith, eliminating them where they serve no good end, honoring them when they serve as a means of enhancing human rights.

In recent years Western churches have become increasingly aware of the degree to which they have looked on churches in other lands as "missions" long after they have become churches in their own right. This has led to an "internationalization of mission." We acknowledge each other as partners in mission, equally Christ's and equally responsible to fulfill the mission mandate. Traffic back and forth between our peoples has increased. In America our parishes have begun to meet magnificent Christian people from Asia, Africa, and Latin America. It is no longer only our people who go to teach in "mission" schools. Now our colleges and seminaries are receiving teachers from what once were "mission" churches. We no longer launch new missionary activity unilaterally. We go as partners in mission with other church bodies closer to the scene. We no longer go with the assumption that our people will be in charge of the work. That will be worked out in the situation. Many are the American Christians who have found themselves working under the leadership of brothers and sisters from the younger churches. God has not established a caste system among his churches. We are all his stewards, seeking to find the ways to most effectively bring the Gospel to all nations.

In some instances the church must bide its time while awaiting missionary opportunity. This is especially true in countries where religious freedom is not a reality. Vast areas of the globe, including billions of people, come under that category today. The most obvious are China and Russia and a number of countries where the Islamic religion holds sway. The churches support whatever limited Christian work is allowed in those lands. They further support a variety of international efforts aimed at universal religious freedom. Study programs are maintained so that there will be knowledgable Christians ready if the doors should open. Dialog is encouraged as a way to keep some channels open. And the Christian faithful are encouraged to pray patiently and constantly that the doors may be open for the Gospel proclamation.

I am preparing this sermon while meeting with the Lutheran World Federation executive committee. We come together as Christians from all parts of the earth. Our clothes differ, our customs differ, our histories differ, our colors differ, and we speak a babel of languages. Yet, we together seek direction from our one Lord as to how to be obedient to his missionary mandate. We function as one fellowship with one mandate even as we come from all over the world. We are your representatives, members of churches brought into being by missionaries past. Now we are the missionaries present, God's people for this day, responding to that same unchanging word, "Go, make disciples of all nations."

God's word for today calls you to make certain Christ's church is always a missionary church.

Amen.

Go—
Baptize

Go therefore and make disciples of all nations, baptizing them in the name of the Father and of the Son and of the Holy Spirit.

(Matthew 28:19)

Baptized into Life With God

Baptism is God's grace announcing that, "You are mine, you belong to me." It is his way of bestowing on you his family name; hence you are baptized ". . . in the name of the Father, and of the Son, and of the Holy Spirit." In baptism God adopts you as his child and makes you his heir. Baptism is God's way of washing away your sins. It is his way of breathing into you the breath of eternal life. In baptism you share in Christ's death. You are able to say that your sinful self has died with Christ in baptism. You can, figuratively, see your sins being nailed in Christ's body on the cross. In baptism you also share in Christ's resurrection life, rising out of the water into the newness of life. In short, baptism is the way by which God gives you himself and his salvation.

Baptized Into Life in the Church

In baptism God not only claims you for himself, however. He also makes you a member of the Christian church. Life as a child of God is never simply a love affair between God and you. He always joins you to his people. The Christian faith is cruciform. The upright pole of the cross signifies God's vertical attachment to you through Christ. The crossarm signifies the horizontal attachment to the members of the church, again through Christ. When you are sealed with God's name, you are joined to all those brothers and sisters who have received the same family name in the same way.

The Scriptures use several pictures to describe this close horizontal baptismal relationship. You are a member in Christ's body, knit together with all those other members, with Christ as the head. In baptism God has made you a child in his eternal family, one of many sisters and brothers. In baptism God has given you irrevocable citizenship papers in his everlasting kingdom. You can renounce that citizenship and leave his kingdom, but from God's side baptism means that the gates of the kingdom are always open. Through baptism God makes it possible for you to say every day in your life, "I belong to God. I belong to God's family, the communion of saints, the one, holy, Christian, apostolic church."

You do not get to choose the other members of the family. As your earthly brothers and sisters are simply given you, so also it is in the church. God gives you those brothers and sisters. You may not always like his choices. Of course, others may look at you and say the same. In any event God has not made you judge over his family. You are to take the brothers and sisters God gives you, in your local congregation and in the church at large. He gives them to you to love, not because they are always lovable or deserving of love, but because God loves them and asks you to do the same.

Look around you. These others gathered in Christ's church are your brothers and sisters. They too have known the waters of baptism. That *is* all you need know about them. Those in your local community of faith are a small part of the total family of God. That is where the family begins for you, however. Old and young, sick and well, noble saints and classic sinners, babes in the faith and mature persons in Christ, they all belong to you and you to them. Together you belong to the church. Together you are the church. It is for you to accept each other, forgive each other, encourage each other, build each other up, and join each other in building Christ's church. Together you are to surround each new baptized child of the family with your earnest prayers and active concern.

The Pilgrim People

It is a pilgrim people to whom God has joined you through baptism. You are a member of the Israel of God, on the march to the promised land. You travel by faith, not by sight. You live on the promise that Christ will move out ahead of you guarding over you in your journeys. There are no space ships or reconnaissance planes to send ahead to the promised land to bring back reports. God's Word is your report—God's Word that tells of the one who has gone across death's boundaries and returned. It is the risen, returned Lord Jesus Christ in whose paths we follow. He is the one who assures us that the road is worth following, that the promised land is there and that it is good.

The journey often leads through difficult wilderness wanderings. God has not promised his children a cakewalk. Often faith's eyes see through a glass darkly and we know not which way to go. There are always golden calves beckoning us to leave the struggle and return to a simple love for money and property and things. There are always enemies seeking to separate us from Christ and his church. Sometimes we stray off, like foolish lambs, and only the Good Shepherd's haunting cry calls us back to the pilgrim flock.

Surrounded by the Saints

We never travel alone on our journey to the promised land, no matter how lonely we sometimes feel. We are surrounded by those other pilgrims following the way in this and other lands. When they seem to have disappeared, we are still surrounded by all those saints of all ages of whom the Scriptures speak. Abraham and Sarah, Ruth and Boaz, Paul and Peter, Martha and Mary, Martin and Katie, and all your grandmothers and grandfathers in the faith, all the saints and martyrs and ordinary Christians who have gone on ahead are there cheering you on, pointing to the Lord Jesus Christ and shouting their encouragement across the centuries.

A Life That Counts

In baptism God calls you to discipleship on the journey to the homeland. He not only wants you as a member of the family, he wants you to live a life that counts. He not only seeks to shower you with his gifts, he sends you out to fulfill your mission. "Go make disciples," he says. You are his messengers to a lost and straying humanity. You are to sound his shepherd's voice to uncertain, unhappy people. The church of Jesus Christ is always a church of witness. Sometimes we are mighty poor witnesses, but there is never anything but our sinfulness to keep us from being a people excitedly declaring the power and love of Christ. You are to invite, urge, persuade, convince people to receive the forgiving love of God.

Discipleship is done with deeds as well as words. God calls his baptized children to be merciful. You are always surrounded by hurting people. Christ charges you to help them. As a result of that charge the church maintains a world service unit to bring food to the hungry, agricultural assistance to those whose land is barren, education to those without schools, and health care to those ridden with disease. That is why you are asked to share in a social service ministry to the aged and infirm, to refugees and to emotionally disturbed youth, retarded children, and alcoholic adults.

God also calls his baptized children to do justice. The world is full of prejudice. The world is full of oppression. We build walls of hatred and prejudice, seeking privilege for ourselves at the expense of others. God's word is that we do justice. We are to organize society so that liberty and justice are the birthright of all. We are to refuse to accept prejudice and hatred and the inevitable polarization they bring. We are to build bridges, not walls. We are to find the ways to make positive contact between rich and poor, between Indian and Black and white and Latin and Oriental. We are to insist that laws, ordinances and practices deal justly with all, with rights of citizenship meaning the same thing for all.

Sharing the Gifts

All that we have talked about here happens because you are baptized. God seeks to share his gifts with everybody. That is why he says to you, to me, to the whole Christian church, "Go . . . baptize." He wants every person to hear him say, "You are mine, you belong to me." He wants every person to experience his undeserved, utterly gracious love. He wants every person to know the joy of being an heir to God's everlasting kingdom.

When you carry your child to the baptismal font, you respond to Christ's charge to "go . . . baptize." So also when you invite others to share the faith. So also when you share in the support of all those pastors and missionaries who on behalf of Christ and the church do the physical acts of baptism. God asks you to use all of your creative gifts to bring others to baptism. Do what you can to bring all whom you can to where they receive the water of life freely.

Two little sisters, seven and eight, were once traveling unattended on a train. They ran about happily, laughing and making friends. They were thoroughly at home and supremely self-confident. On their dresses were pinned tags with their names, the names of their parents, and their destination. They could be happy and free because they knew who they were, they knew to whom they belonged, and they knew where they were going.

That is what Christ does for you in baptism. He puts his sign on you so that you will always know who you are, to whom you belong, and where you are going. He has equipped you for your journey. God asks you to help the same thing happen to others. He calls you to care about them, all of them out there. He calls you to be one member of the great church of Christ who hears Christ's word, "Go, therefore, and make disciples, baptizing . . ."

Amen.

Go—
Teaching Them
to Observe

Go therefore and make disciples . . . teaching them to observe all that I have commanded you. (Matthew 28:19-20)

There is great celebration in heaven and earth when a person becomes a member of the body of Christ. Whether infant or adult the new member is an occasion of joy for all of God's people. Perhaps you have known the thrill of holding your child at the font as the water and word brought life and salvation to the flesh of your flesh. You may have shared the ecstasy of a grown person kneeling, fighting with doubts, and speaking the words of faith as the heart was warmed by the love of Christ. You may have experienced in your own life the apparently random sequence of events that brought you one day to say from the heart, "I believe in God the Father almighty . . . and in Jesus Christ his only son our Lord . . . and in the Holy Spirit."

The entry ceremony into the family of God is not the end of the matter, however. The Christian life does not stop with conversion or with baptism. There is, nevertheless, the temptation to have it so. Life in the church can become static, even perfunctory. The church can become a place where you are baptized, married, and buried. The rest of life you shift for yourself, following whatever inclinations move you.

Or if your entry into the household of God was a particularly emotional experience, there is the temptation to keep trading on that experience. You can tell about it again and again; and when that wears thin, you can seek to repeat the experience. There are those in the family of faith for whom the repeated conversion experience becomes a sort of insulin shot, a charging of the emotions, starting the spiritual adrenalin running anew.

From Infancy to Maturity

The word of our Lord Jesus takes note of these possibilities when he tells us to "go make disciples, teaching them to observe all that I have commanded you." Christian rebirth is the beginning. Then, as with the newborn infant, comes the process of growing up. It would be cruel and wrong if we were to rejoice at the birth of a new child and then leave it to shift for itself. The newborn requires care, love, nurture. It is not able to be an adult the first day of birth. No more can the child, of whatever age, who is a newborn disciple of Christ. That is one of the reasons the church has often designated "sponsors" for the newly baptized. It is recognition that the new Christian needs encouragement, example, instruction in God's Word, and friendship.

Thus the Lord Jesus commands us to make disciples by teaching — "teaching to observe all things." This sets before us the whole of the Bible. It is our function to teach each other to trust God, to worship God, and to serve God, all according to the Scriptures.

Teaching to Trust

Human life is to be centered in God. It is the life and activity of God that claims our faith. The Scriptures are our basic resource. They are first and foremost the record of God's dealings with his people. They provide an inexhaustible series of texts from which one's faith in God is deepened, broadened, and strengthened.

Hence it is that the Christian family is always

placing before its children the Word of the living God. That Word of God is both simple enough for the simplest to trust and more complex than the most learned can comprehend. Whatever our level of comprehension, we are all called to teach each other to trust God. Parents are given special responsibilities to teach their children. Congregations appoint pastors and teachers to assist in special ways. It is not expected that everyone will be able to teach everything, but no one is excluded from the charge to teach as he or she is able.

We teach the smallest child to sing "Jesus loves me," and no matter how learned or sophisticated we become, we never stop singing that. We do, however, continue to expand endlessly the meaning of the words, "Jesus loves me." We help each other discover the deep truth that God is triune—Father, Son and Spirit. We declare the majesty and mystery of God who is with us always and yet maintains dominion over absolutely everything that is. We teach each other to observe how God our creator has been busy throughout human history calling to himself a people who will trust, worship, and serve him. We never cease describing how "God was in Christ, reconciling the world to himself." We teach of that amazing grace by which Almighty God, through Jesus of Nazareth, became one with his sinful and perverse human family. We feed each other's faith with the Gospel, the good news about God, recorded in those matchless words from the voices and pens of the prophets and apostles. We teach of the mighty Spirit of God who lays claim to our hearts and bestows upon us life's greatest gifts. Our growing faith keeps filling in the gaps between the knowledge that in the beginning of life it is God who creates us, in the center of life it is God who through Christ redeems us, and at the end of life it is God who receives us unto himself.

It is because of the inexhaustible character of God and his Word that Lutherans have practiced a "catechetical evangelism." There is content to the Christian faith. There is a history through which God has spoken. The immortal, invisible God has made himself known to faith. He keeps on expanding faith's knowledge through the teaching work of his people. Luther wrote a Small Catechism that has served as a basic tool of Christian instruction for millions of God's children. It remains a useful help in "teaching them to observe all that I have commanded you."

The Christian church has always put a high premium on a learned laity and a learned clergy. The school has been a constant companion of the church. Certainly that has been true of Lutheran Christians. We declare the importance of continuing Christian education with our church schools, Bible schools, with outstanding Christian colleges, and with superior seminaries. We will not make the Christian life exclusively into an educational program, but neither will we forget Christ's ongoing charge to "teach them to observe."

Teaching to Worship

Christian faith is not only the inward reception of God and growth in Christian comprehension. It is also a faith that moves outward in worship and service. We show our love of God in acts of worship and in loving service to others.

Christians worship God. That is the way we describe our loving response to him. Worship encompasses all of life, but we speak here of those actions in which we consciously offer ourselves to God in acts of worship. We teach each other to worship not so much by formal instruction as by sharing our worship. Most of us learn best by doing. So we pray together, sing hymns of praise together, study the Scriptures together, share Word and Sacraments together, and offer our tithes together. We breathe our native air, receive the bread of life, and grow to healthy maturity as we find ourselves together—God's sinful, forgiven people—together in worship. It is because of this taught and caught worship experience that it is always good Christian evangelism to invite others to come to church with you. Serious, joyful Christian worship is an impressive witness to the lordship of God. It reaches the heart.

Regular participation in corporate worship is both a duty and a delight. We need the discipline of duty to keep reminding us that our face is to be turned toward God. Without a sense of duty and discipline we tend to lose our sense of direction. Worship should also be a delight. Worship provides us with forms by which we can corporately give heartfelt expression to love for God and his people. Of course, we can make worship bland and lifeless. We are capable of doing that with all of God's gifts. It need not be so, however, and it should not be so. Christians have always expressed the joy of faith in Christ through prayer, songs of praise, giving, and sharing. The forms of worship have been worked out through centuries of Christian experience. They are vehicles by which humans can express their faith in worship.

It is good and right that you let your heart speak when you gather for worship. Open your hearts to God's love for you and offer him your love in return. In your prayers and in your songs and in your handshakes offer your love to your neighbor and open your heart to be loved in return. Then those worship hours will become treasures as well as duties.

Teaching to Serve

Faith active in love involves also the worship of God with our daily deeds. Christ calls for followers. Discipleship means free, self-given obedience in response to the summons of Christ. The Spirit of God is given us not only that we might be rescued by the forgiving love of Christ, not only to be held as babes in God's everlasting arms, but also to grow up and give him mature allegiance. Christ calls us to be who we are without settling for what we are. He sends us out into the world with the charge that we not become worldly but that we help the world become godly.

There is no honest way to avoid the call of Christ to costly service. He calls us to love, to serve, and that always claims a high price. The call to a discipleship of serving is simply there for us to observe and to teach others to observe. He says, "If any man would come after me, let him deny himself and take up his cross and follow me. For whoever would save his life will lose it, and whoever loses his life for my sake will find it. For what will it profit a man, if he gains the whole world and forfeits his life? Or what shall a man give in return for his life?"

Christian discipleship calls for single-minded allegiance. Instead of allegiance to any form of self-interest, our allegiance is to the Lord Jesus Christ. Instead of looking to be served, we are called to offer ourselves as servants. Instead of battling for personal privilege, we are called to battle for justice. Instead of insisting on personal rights, we are called to insist on human rights. Instead of loving things and using people, we are called to love people and use things. Instead of treating God's creation as a private preserve for human exploitation, we are to be stewards of his estates. Instead of passing by on the other side we are to minister to the needs of those battered by life's misfortunes. God's Word puts it to us simply. ". . . for he who does not love his brother whom he has seen, cannot love God whom he has not seen."

Love is no simple inner feeling. Love is doing. God does not only want us to receive his love. He wants us to help make a world full of loving people. And not only that. He calls us to organize our society in such a way that its laws and structures assure justice and dignity for all. That is the way that love translates itself into the governance of human society.

Teaching — A Tall Order

Now, teaching each other to observe all that God has commanded is a tall order. It is never completed even if we teach each other to trust God, to worship God, and to serve God. The Spirit of God keeps on prodding us to an ever more complete maturity. We would soon give up in despair were it not for God's unending willingness to forgive us as we struggle to be disciples. He encourages us by making it clear to us that discipleship is always to a life that counts. There is joy in knowing the battle is worth fighting.

Figure out where the call to discipleship takes you. To what kind of servanthood are you summoned? How do you give your life away for Christ's sake? How do you spend yourself for the sake of others? How do you devote yourself to ensuring justice for the oppressed? How do you show mercy to people broken in body, mind, and spirit? How do you encourage, strengthen, and build up those who are closest to you? How do you devote yourself to a partner in marriage, to maintaining a family that is secure and strong in the face of societal storms?

Perhaps you will not find answers to all those questions. You will find enough answers, however, to keep yourself busy for life. You will have taught others to observe what God commands even if you only help them to wrestle with those questions. *Go therefore and make disciples . . . teaching them to observe all that I have commanded you.* *Amen.*

Go—
I Am with You Always

Go therefore and make disciples . . . and lo, I am with you always. (Matthew 28:19-20)

The world is full of nostrums designed to make us feel happily at home in the universe. Advertisements pour across our desks and across television screens assuring us that one remedy or another will correct our ills and send us on our way rejoicing. Sometimes it is pills for our nasal passages or iron for our tired blood. Sometimes it is clothes or cosmetics or deodorants that will make us desirable to others. Sometimes it is a new technique that will assure us of success and satisfaction in our work.

In recent days there have been many attractive offers to help you "realize your human potential" or "develop your psychic energy" or "find personal fulfillment." A whole bevy of practitioners have appeared with schools and retreats and religious movements that assure you of finding a key "something" that has been missing. This is no new phenomenon. Humans have always been ingenious in finding cures for human ailments. For some sinful reason it is difficult to lay hold of that which God has given to make his people well.

Nevertheless, the Christian church keeps plugging along in response to that incredible word, "Go, make disciples . . . I am with you always." It is God that we need. It is God who through Christ has given himself to us.

The Practice of the Presence

Way back in the Middle Ages a lay brother in a monastery wrote a little tract called *The Practice of the Presence of God*. Brother Lawrence was his name and he was a cook in a monastery kitchen. He was not one of the monks devoted to scholarship or formal piety. He was in charge of the kitchen, a busy place not designed for quiet study or prayerful contemplation. Yet Brother Lawrence made it a holy place. He wrote down how he practiced the presence of God while making the kitchen hum. His little tract has lived on to bless millions. Brother Lawrence discovered how to practice the presence of God while cooking the meals, washing the pots and pans, talking with visitors, walking in the garden and going to bed at night. There were no gimmicks, no new tricks. He took seriously the promise God freely bestows on all who will hear him. "Lo, I am with you always, to the close of the age." Then he offered his work and his life as witness to the love of God for ordinary people.

God makes no restrictions on the promise of his presence. Not "when you are good" nor "when things are going well." The Psalmist caught the wonder of this word when he wrote:

Whither shall I go from thy Spirit?
Or whither shall I flee from thy presence?
If I ascend to heaven, thou art there!
If I make my bed in Sheol, thou art there!
(Psalm 139:7-8)

Actually the promise of God's presence is a hard thing if one prefers not to be known. In Friedrich Nietzsche's book, *Thus Spake Zarathustra,* a character known only as "the ugliest man" murders God. The death of God was accomplished in order that no one, not even God, would know the truth about the ugliest man. It was bad enough living with oneself in secret. To know that someone else knew what you were really like—that was intolerable. If we live in darkness, unwilling to have our lives forgiven and changed, then the presence of God is indeed a threat rather than a blessing.

For the Christian summoned to be God's witness, however, the word is pure blessing. God does not come to condemn us for our shortcomings. He comes with forgiveness, encouragement, and the assurance of his constant care no matter how much we may bungle things.

God's Use of Your Witness

It is, finally, the convincing presence of God that makes it possible for you to bear convincing witness to others. You do not convert anybody. God does that. He uses your witness as the opportunity for his Spirit. He does not depend on your brilliance, cleverness, or skill. He uses your exhortations, your preaching, your inviting, your concern, and your loyalty, but without his active presence your words would be of no effect.

It is for that reason that God attaches this promise of his presence to the charge, "Go, make disciples." He does not send you out alone. Your witness to the crucified and risen Lord Jesus Christ will work the miracle of faith because of the convincing Spirit of God, not because of the convincing weight of your words. You make your witness, therefore, not depending on yourself for

Go—I Am with You Always

results, but depending on God. If your witness bears no apparent fruit, it is not because of your failure, neither because of God's failure, but because people are free to refuse the Spirit's work.

That should make you bold in witnessing to the words and work of Christ. What matter if someone thinks you are a bit balmy. The Lord is with you. What if your zeal for the Gospel leaves you off the list for some social event? The Lord is with you. What if you feel inadequate and strange in speaking of Christ and his kingdom? The Lord is with you.

Now obviously God is not asking his witnesses to be blundering fools, using inappropriate times to blurt out their witness. The research scientist serves God in reporting his latest scientific findings without using it as an occasion to sneak in a testimony. The cook serves God with his cooking even if it does not afford occasion for witnessing to his customers. The researcher is not always delivering learned papers, however, nor is the cook always over his stove. The occasions for witness arise in everyone's life. You can be alert to the opportunities that appear in natural ways. You can be wise enough to create opportunities as well. After all, you are not looking for an opportunity to hurt or trick a person. You have opportunity to be the means by which God bestows himself, his forgiveness, life and salvation on people who need him above everything else.

The stories of God's effective witnesses abound. They inevitably involve the awareness of living in his presence. After Jesus' death the disciples were a quiet and dispirited group until they discovered him in their midst. Then there was nothing short of death that could stop their telling of Christ's lordship.

God Works in Various Ways

There is no telling when or how it is that the living presence of God becomes known to a person. The Spirit blows where he wills is the biblical way of declaring that mystery. All we can say is that it happens as a result of the telling and retelling of the Gospel story. It happens in those baptismal services where the water joins the word. Sometimes it is in a worship gathering where everyone knows the Word is to be preached. Sometimes it is as two or three walk on the way to a meeting, as on the road to Emmaus. Sometimes it is like Phillip and the Ethiopian poring over the Scriptures together. For one, awareness of the living God comes when quiet and alone; for another, when the shells of war are screaming overhead. Some can never remember a time when God's presence was not lively and real for them.

I remember vividly attending a meeting of the David Hume Society at the University of Edinburgh. As David Hume's name would suggest, the group was made up of agnostic students seeking after truth. The speaker was the noted theologian and teacher, Principal John Baillie of New College, Edinburgh. He gave a marvelous account of the Christian faith. Then, after a lively period of debate, one of the students asked him when he had come to believe that Jesus Christ was both Lord and living. Dr. Baillie's reply was: "I clearly recollect events back to the age of two, and I cannot remember a time when I did not believe that Jesus Christ was alive and Lord. I believe he came to me in baptism and now I am 72 years old and he has never left me." It was a quiet group of agnostics who left that night.

God's Use of Disciples' Deeds

The call to witness is not only a call to verbal testimony. Neither is the promise of God's presence only for those occasions of verbal witness. There have been thousands of occasions when believers have silently borne witness and then prayed as did our Lord on the cross, "Father, into your hands I commend my spirit." Think of the eras of persecution when people were made to kneel before the emperor or face execution. Somehow there were Christians who refused to bend the knee. Their witness was not lost even though they lost their lives. So effective was their witness in fact, that it led Tertullian to declare, "The blood of the martyrs is the seed of the church."

Only a few years ago a band of people knelt in prayer with Martin Luther King on the sidewalk of an American city. They were protesting cruel and inhuman injustice worked on black Americans. They knelt with the words ringing in their ears that "the Lord is your shield and protector." Night sticks fell on hurting heads and jail was the immediate result, but they were made strong to witness for justice in the knowledge the Lord was with them. Who knows how many hearts were moved to discipleship by such bold acts of witness.

The making of disciples comes from innumerable forms of witness. Sometimes the witness is planned and sometimes it is spontaneous. Sometimes you have the warm, inner feeling of God's presence. You just sense that he is present. You feel it with every fiber of your being. On such feelings, however, you cannot depend. Human feelings are notoriously untrustworthy. You may next feel that God has deserted you and left you utterly alone. You are to trust in his promise, not

Go—I Am with You Always

in your feelings. The Word of God alone is sure. Whatever your feelings at any given moment, you are to bring to your consciousness that strong word of the Lord Jesus, "Lo I am with you always." Trust that word, and then go out boldly to make your witness. God has not left you to make disciples by yourself. He sends you out with a message from on high, and he sends you with the promise of his presence. *Go therefore and make disciples . . . and lo, I am with you always.*

Amen.

Go—
to the Close of the Age

Go therefore and make disciples ... and lo, I am with you always, to the close of the age."
(Matthew 28:19-20)

The "Now" Generation

It is popular to call this the "now" generation. The suggestion is that people in large numbers are grasping life's sensations moment by moment, each sensation accepted by itself unattached to past or future. The past is viewed with guilt, with a sense of failure. The future is viewed with foreboding, with a sense that things may get even worse. Hence comes the inclination to do away with both past and future. Live now! Grasp the fruits of life available to you right now! Let his-

Go—to the Close of the Age 69

tory render what judgments it will about the past and the future. A person's time to live is—now!

Implicit in such a "now" view is the assumption that any moment provides opportunities for pleasurable sensations. It is not just any kind of "now" that is anticipated, but one that provides pleasure. The credit card is an ingenious American accommodation to the "now" style of life. "Buy now—pay later" is the slogan. "Why wait to enjoy life?" ask the advertisements. Why, indeed, when all that is necessary is a plastic credit card that fits in a machine and sends you home with desires immediately gratified.

Events during a recent recession illustrate the degree to which the "now" generation is a reality. The energy crisis, high unemployment and galloping inflation combined to cause great uncertainty about past practices and future possibilities. One would have thought there would be a careful, prudent, belt-tightening reaction among the citizenry. Instead there was an unprecedented run on entertainment spending. Resorts were booked far in advance. Vacation travel increased. Luxury items sold well. Pleasure was bought—now!

Already a generation ago Pastor Dietrich Bonhoeffer, from his Nazi prison cell, called attention to the pastoral difficulties with such an attitude. He wrote, "The man who has no urge to do his duty to the past and to shape the future is a man without a memory, and there seems no way of getting hold of such a person and bringing him to his senses. Every word, even if it impresses him for a moment, goes in one ear and out the other. What is to be done about him? It is a tremendous pastoral problem this." (*Prisoner for God*, p. 99)

Christ's people can keep offering an option. We can, with words and deeds, keep calling attention to a much richer, more fulfilling way of living now. Far from attempting to eliminate the past and future in order to live now, we claim the past and the future. We do so with confidence, trusting in God who is Lord of the past and the future and the right now. What need is there to fear or hide a past and future when we hear with faith the word of our Lord Jesus, "Lo, I am with you always, to the close of the age"?

A Good Look at the Past

Human fulfillment is not to be found in an unending quest for pleasurable experiences. We are made for life with God. Our highest fulfillment is to be found in trusting, loving, worshiping, and serving him. We can look at the past and see not only human folly and failures, but the mighty acts of God. When seen thus it is Christ's cross that rises high over the human past. Through that cross we see God coming as a suffering servant to share our human joys and sorrows and to carry our human sin. Christians do not have all the explanations as to why history is as it is. We do claim enough understanding to trust him who has said to us, "Fear not, for I am with you." Our hearts tell us the truth of that towering statement, "God was in Christ reconciling the world to himself."

If there were no Christ in that backward look there would be cause for despair. Yes, there would be great human achievement in a realistic look at the past. Overlaying that achievement, however, would be the relentless reality of human sin, suffering and death. Death would always have the last word. If we only saw Christ going to the cross as humanity's sacrificial lamb, we would have to view his life also as another noble human effort that ended with death. Had he simply disappeared in death his name would have been no more than another footnote in human history. Christ rose from the dead, however, and his cross has become a symbol not only of his death but of his resurrection life. We look at the past through Christ's cross and see not only the sacrificial lamb but also the conquering king. Through Christ's cross the past becomes the arena not of human achievement or failure, but the arena of God's steadfast, loving, redemptive pursuit of his people. Forget the past? Not on your life! The past discloses the crucified, risen Christ, him who says to us in every now—"lo, I am with you always."

A Good Look at the Future

That same Christ goes on to say "I am with you to the close of the age." He is the Lord of the future as well as of the past and the present. You who trust him will not be overwhelmed with fear of the future. You may know precious little about future earthly events, but you can know two things that enable you to look to the future with confidence. Christ has promised to be with you always; and Christ has secured an eternal kingdom for his people. That is what he means when he says he will be with you to the close of the age.

The church's confidence in the future God has prepared finds expression in credal form. "I believe in the resurrection of the body and in the life everlasting" we confess in the Apostles' Creed. There is no way to make that confession without looking to the future. The words provide us with a way of declaring our faith that Jesus Christ has assured a good future for his people. It is our way of saying that we claim citizenship, through the grace of our Lord Jesus Christ, in the kingdom not of this world. It is our way of saying that no matter when or how the close of this age comes Christ will gather his believing family in an eternal household. It is faith's way of saying we will meet the end of earthly life in the confidence that Christ has indeed "gone to prepare a place for us."

In Christ the past, present, and future meet. He makes it possible to say in every present moment "now is the time of salvation." Through faith in him we are able to affirm the past. It is the arena of his activity. Through past actions he has assured the future. His promise to be with us *now* means that he brings with him both past and future glory. Now we are allowed, through faith in him, to share in his death and resurrection. Now, through faith in him, we can share by foretaste life in the kingdom he has won. The full excitement of living now is reserved for those who through Christ can claim both past and future with joy.

Evangelical Outreach — Right to the End

The word of our Lord calls us to "go make disciples . . . to the close of the age." It is not enough that we claim the fruits of Christ's past and future life. We are to share what we have received. We are to share Christ's urgency that everyone "be saved and come to the knowledge of the truth." We are to tell the story of God's love through

Christ to anyone who will listen. We are to pray and work and serve and make visits and invite whomsoever we can to join Christ's fellowship of believers.

The urgency of witness is to be maintained whatever the circumstances. Christ's life and love is for little children and old people. His grace is to be shared in times of trial and times of ease. If we were to receive word that the world's end was to come tomorrow we would be compelled by our faith to go make disciples until the end comes. If we were to receive word the world was to live another 10 million years our faith would still compel us to go make disciples until the end comes. In season and out, when times are good and when they are bad, when we feel like it and when we do not, when we are young and foolish and when we are old and foolish, we are to be witnesses of God's Christ, seeking to make disciples.

We have no way of knowing when or how the grace of God will reach in to claim for Christ a person's heart. Charles Williams, a superb theologian who wove his witness into plays and poems and novels, wrote a delightful little play called "Grab and Grace." All of the play's characters reflected their names. They were all predictable in their actions, especially the one called "Grab." There was one exception, "Grace." He was utterly unpredictable. He burst in at a funeral, for in-

Go—to the Close of the Age

stance, playing a flute and dancing a happy jig until it was no longer possible to be sad and gloomy. He simply showed up, kind and generous, to bestow his goodness and mercy wherever he saw fit.

So it is with the grace of God. We cannot know where, how, or when he will use our witness to his power and love. We do have his promise that he *will* use our witness. Hence we can trust his grace, not only to renew us in the faith day by day, but also to use even our inadequate witness to give birth to faith in others.

You are Christ's people, friends. He has bestowed on you his blessing and called you to be his witnesses. He sends you out today with his promise, "Lo, I am with you always." What sins of the past can stand up against that? What worries about the future hold a candle to that? What better promise could God give you for full and fine life, right now? How better could God equip you to "go make disciples . . . to the close of the age"?

There is more than one way to live in a "now" generation. Christ has set before you his way. Make it your way. Now!

Amen.

Part Two

REFLECTIONS

on

Evangelical Outreach

What Is Evangelical Outreach?

It is possible to define evangelical outreach both broadly and narrowly. The broad definition includes everything the people of God do in response to the Word of God. The narrow definition includes only those actions explicitly directed toward making Christ known to an unbelieving world. Each definition has its vigorous advocates. It is not necessary, however, to choose one or the other. Both definitions can be held simultaneously, therefore assuring a dynamic tension that is essential to life in the church.

When that tension is not maintained, the people of God spend an undue amount of time debating whether the church's proper task is evangelism or social action, proclaiming the Gospel or doing works of love. One side will contend that evangelism is properly everything the church does in response to God's Word. The other side will argue that evangelism is only the active, verbal proclamation of the gospel. The one side is tempted to minimize the central importance of verbal Gospel proclamation by claiming witness for everything the church does. The other side is tempted to identify so exclusively with gospel proclamation that faith fails to become active in love. Either way the fulness of Christian life and witness suffers.

The broad task of mission is to acknowledge the Lordship of Christ over all of existence. It is the church's mission to make Christ known to an unbelieving world, to nurture the faithful, to do acts of mercy, to seek justice for all human affairs and to properly steward the gifts of creation. All such acts bear witness to the power and love of God and are integral to the total mission of the church. The wholeness of the church's witness to God is maintained only as God's people are active on all fronts. People whom God seeks to reach will be suspicious of a witness that ignores obviously important elements of human life. It is right, therefore, to insist that the entire response of the people of God is the church's evangelical outreach.

Nevertheless it is necessary for the church to clearly delineate particular tasks and distinguish

What Is Evangelical Outreach

among them. It is one thing to become an advocate for a person unjustly imprisoned. It is another thing to bring a Gospel witness to prisoners whether rightly or wrongly imprisoned. Both ministries are of God, vital elements in the total mission of God's people. On the one hand, however, we seek justice through law. On the other hand we offer God's love in Christ, free and full, whether justice prevails or not.

Lutherans have been particularly insistent that the Scriptures clearly distinguish between the Law and the Gospel. God summons us to discipleship through the Gospel. Faith in the saving work of Christ does not come through the Law's commands to live righteously. As disciples, however, we are required to apply both Gospel and Law to the human situation. It is not possible to bring order and justice to a sinful society simply by proclaiming the Gospel. Neither is it possible to present the transcendant love of God through the Law.

The task of establishing justice in society is not uniquely the responsibility of disciples of Christ. That is the responsibility of all citizens, Christian and non-Christian alike. The charge to "Go, make disciples of all nations, baptizing them in the name of the Father and of the Son and of the Holy Ghost" is uniquely Christian. That is the central charge Christ gave his followers. It is fundamental to the life and work of the church. The church has no allies in this task. The church alone is commissioned to see that it is done.

It is essential, therefore, that we recognize not only the unity but also the difference in the offering of God's eternal grace in the Gospel and working to establish earthly justice through the Law.

Thus it is right and proper to speak of a "narrow" definition of evangelical outreach. The New Testament church gives vivid illustration of the primacy attached to making the Gospel known. The early disciples did not ignore the needs of orphans and widows. When famine brought hunger to the people, they did their best to feed them. They worked at establishing a just and peaceful society. Overriding all such emphases, however, was the concern that all might know Christ. They went out looking for people whom they could tell about Christ. Peter and John risked their lives in order to preach on the temple steps. Stephen left his deacon's work and was martyred for preaching the Gospel. Philip climbed into a chariot with an Ethiopian official in order to tell him about Christ. Paul devoted himself to knowing only Christ crucified, telling the good news whenever anyone would listen, in jails, synagogues and town halls. Lydia gladly

What Is Evangelical Outreach   83

left her garment shop to participate in the work of the Gospel.

They cared passionately that Christ be known, loved, and trusted. They told of his words and his works, his suffering, death, and resurrection. They proclaimed his victory over sin, death, and Satan. They called people to repentance and invited them to share life in Christ's kingdom through faith in him. They taught and preached and prayed and baptized, all in the name of the Lord Jesus. They provided the backdrop for all subsequent life in the Christian church.

Each following generation has been given the same fundamental responsibility for making known the love of Christ. Evangelical outreach is an apt and descriptive title for the work assigned to the church. Evangelical outreach is telling people of God's redeeming acts. It is making known the life and words of Jesus of Nazareth. It is declaring the death and resurrection and everlasting Lordship of Jesus Christ. Evangelical outreach is explicitly inviting people to share in the life of Christ and his church.

Evangelical outreach in this sense does not include the whole mission of the church. It concentrates on the central element of that mission. Proclaiming the Gospel is not the only way of showing God's love for his people. It is the indispensable way of showing that love.

In summary, it is useful to define evangelical outreach broadly so long as it is also defined narrowly. Evangelical outreach properly includes the whole mission of the church to the whole world so long as it maintains a central focus on telling the whole world of God's love in Christ. The intent of this book, and the intent of a Lutheran emphasis on evangelical outreach, is to strengthen the whole mission by giving special emphasis once more to the central mission. This we do in direct response to the Word of God that admonishes us to "go, make disciples."

Lutheran Identity and Witness

American Lutheran churches resulted from the massive emigration of hundreds of thousands of Lutherans from Europe to the United States. Some left their homelands because of economic necessity, some came to America to find religious freedom, others simply caught the "America fever." The Lutheran immigration became substantial in the 18th century, peaked in the last half of the 19th century, and continued through the first quarter of the 20th century. A considerable influx of Lutherans from the Baltic countries and Hungary occurred after World War II. Otherwise the last 50 years have seen the end of immigrant boats with large numbers of Lutherans.

An Immigrant Church

Throughout the immigrant period and for some years thereafter, Lutheran evangelical outreach was largely a matter of gathering Lutheran immigrants and their descendants. Lay leaders and circuit-riding pastors gathered together a particular ethnic group, began worship services and instruction of the young, called a permanent pastor, and another Lutheran congregation was formed. The use of old-country language and the geographic clustering according to country of origin made it difficult for members of a congregation to reach out beyond their particular ethnic group.

That pattern continued to hold even after the language difference disappeared. United States Lutherans developed prospect lists and started new congregations by finding people with a Lutheran background. The movement of second and third generation Lutherans from one part of the country to another made this possible and even necessary. Now, however, a new day has arrived. The immigrant boats have stopped. The descendants of Lutheran immigrants are scattering all over the land. The family and cultural ties which bound people to their German, Norwegian, Swedish, Danish, Finnish, Latvian, Hungarian, and Slovakian churches are disappearing. The Americanizing of Lutheran immigrant families is an accomplished fact. An evangelical outreach strategy geared only to people of Lutheran background is clearly inadequate today. It has served its purpose but now it must be left behind.

Lutheran evangelical outreach at its best has never been satisfied only with reaching people of Lutheran background. Plain-spoken Christian people have been God's instruments for making congregation after congregation reflect the many ethnic backgrounds of the American population. Congregations slowly become smaller and weaker when this does not happen. The time has come when broad-scale Christian witness must be the work of every congregation that will remain vital and strong. It is important that today's Lutherans understand and appropriate those elements of the Lutheran heritage that endure regardless of cultural changes. It is such enduring elements that should inform evangelical outreach efforts from Lutheran congregations.

The Enduring Heritage

It was not just ethnic heritage that kept Lutherans bound to each other through the immigrant period. Lutherans have always understood themselves as belonging to a confessional church, a church with a distinct theological heritage.

Strong loyalties to doctrine, the sacraments, congregational life and liturgy were decisive in maintaining Lutheran congregations. These emphases have made the Lutheran church attractive to people who do not share a common ethnic heritage. It is through doctrine and practice that Lutherans identify themselves and make their distinctive contributions.

Lutherans have been shaped by a fundamental commitment to the sovereign grace of God. The Lutheran Reformation came into being to assert the basic fact that we are justified by the grace of God alone, appropriated through faith in Jesus Christ. It is God's action that is decisive and not ours. Lutherans are always skittish of Christian movements that put a heavy emphasis on what *people* do. Lutherans believe the focus should always be primarily on what *God* does and only secondarily on people's response. Lutheran hymns tend to have first lines like "A Mighty Fortress Is Our God," or "Built on a Rock the Church Does Stand," rather than "*My* Faith Looks Up to Thee," or "*My* Jesus *I* Love Thee."

Lutherans live in the conviction that all authority has been given to Christ and that his authority is exercised through the Scriptures. It is to the promises of the Scriptures that Lutherans turn for certainty, strength and help. Human judgments and human emotions are to remain

Lutheran Identity and Witness 89

subject to the Scriptural word. During the Reformation period Lutherans were identified as people who held to "Grace alone; faith alone; the word alone." Lutherans readily accept that description today.

The conviction that God's grace is the central point of Christian faith helps explain the Lutheran understanding of the sacraments. Lutherans believe the Scriptures teach baptismal rebirth, that baptism is a gracious act of God to which people respond in faith, that the Holy Spirit is given in baptism, and that baptism is God's promise to us that he will always be our faithful Father. Baptism is God's act in which we trustingly share.

We bring infants to the baptismal font, not in the belief that they will immediately receive mature Christian faith, but in response to God's command and in the confidence that God's Spirit there adopts the child into the family of God. A beginning is made. Subsequently, the child will grow in Christian knowledge and faith toward the goal of maturity in Christ. Family membership is just as real for the infant, however, as for the adult. There are no first and second-class members in God's family. The spiritual process is analogous to our physical birth and growth in our earthly family. People go from infancy to childhood to maturity. Along the way there will be self-conscious decisions as to whether we will stay in the family. Doubts and temptations will be faced. The whole saga of faith, from baptism to death, is the story of the grace of God at work in people, bringing believers from darkness to light, from infancy to maturity, from membership in an earthly family to membership in a heavenly as well as earthly family.

A similar doctrinal view prevails with regard to the Lord's Supper. This is God's act, instituted by Christ himself, by which he feeds and nourishes the faithful. Lutherans believe that Christ is truly present, according to his word, and that he has chosen this means to strengthen our faith and our life together. Partaking of the Lord's Supper is more than a symbolic act by which we remind ourselves of Christ's death and resurrection. It is a means of grace, a means by which the resurrected Christ is present among us, building and strengthening our faith in him and his salvation. It is a simple act by which God again and again makes his presence known to us and strengthens us for each day's duties.

Lutherans take public worship seriously indeed. It is at public worship that the Word is proclaimed, the sacraments administered, and people join in praising God. Worship needs form and structure. It has been wisely said that the only alternative to good liturgical forms are bad

Lutheran Identity and Witness 91

liturgical forms. Because worship is an expression of the Gospel, Lutherans are concerned for forms which both demonstrate an appreciation for our heritage and which give clear expression to the Gospel for our life today.

While Lutherans insist that liturgical rites and ceremonies may vary from place to place and change through the years, we take seriously the liturgical work of centuries of church life. The preaching of the Word, the sharing of the sacraments, and the offerings of tithes, prayer, praise, and thanksgiving have always been integral to the church's life. Musical forms, use of vestments, church architecture, and manner of participation in worship have varied greatly and still do. Lutherans have generally been slow to make liturgical changes. Luther told his followers to change liturgical practices only when there is good reason to do so. That continues to be good advice.

Our worship is a public witness. The faithful gathering of Christian people for worship is a sign in this world of God's presence and dominion. Worship does not end in the sanctuary but continues in the witness and service of God's people in the world. Lutherans have an understanding of the world which gives direction for that witness and service. We understand clearly the tragedy and brokenness of the human situation. We know the pervasive consequences of sin.

Yet we take life in this world seriously, too. We are not called out of the world nor can we abandon the world to Satan and the forces of evil. We are called to bear witness to God's love for the world through Jesus Christ. We are called to care for the earth and our neighbors. We live and serve in the sure and certain hope of that kingdom which God will establish and which is greater than all we can even imagine.

These matters have been at the center of Lutheran self-identity. Apart from them Lutheran immigrants would most likely have been caught up in the Christian churches already flourishing in America. These elements remain essential to the biblical faith. Hence Lutherans continue to believe it important that there be a Lutheran witness within the one, holy, catholic, and apostolic church. Lutheran evangelical outreach will reflect the enduring Lutheran heritage briefly sketched in these pages. The Lutheran contribution to the outreach of the whole Christian church will be most effective when that is so.

A Time to Reach Out

Evangelical outreach is always the task of the Christian church. That is made especially clear in the great commission of Matthew 28:18-20 which serves as the theme for this book. That is only one of many biblical texts calling us to be Christ's witnesses, however. Jesus found many ways to charge his followers to be his witnesses, preachers of the kingdom, proclaimers of the good news of God's love.

Jesus sent his disciples out to witness one by one and two by two. His expressed intent was to make the kingdom of God known to all people. His disciples were sent out to invite everybody to the wedding feast. He gave the outreach task to all those who had been captured by faith in him. In each generation that means the witness responsibility belongs to all of us who call Jesus Lord. It is not the only task he gives us, but it is always the central one. Christ's disciples are to reach people with the good news of God's love through Jesus Christ and invite them to share in the fellowship and service of those who believe. That is evangelical outreach.

A Time to Emphasize

While evangelical outreach is always the church's task, there are times that call for special emphasis. American Lutherans face just such a time. Many things have preoccupied us in recent years. We have been caught in the secularizing rush of twentieth century society. There has been the uncertainty generated by the strong attack on all social institutions, "the establishment," during the late 1960s and early '70s.

There has been persistent questioning about the "viability" or "relevance" of the church in our age. Various social crises have clamored for ethical response—wars and threats of wars, racism, energy shortages, ecological disasters, unemployment, the value of human life, the family farm, and the plight of the inner cities. There has been frustration that the churches have not been able to provide ready answers to such critical problems.

Christian people have been further frustrated because some feel too much effort has been spent in addressing critical social issues and others feel they have received too little attention. When congregations, councils, or conventions address such issues, they are vulnerable to the charge of inadequate concern for spreading the Gospel. When they ignore such issues, they are accused of insensitivity to people's needs. Hence a good deal of energy has been spent in arguing the question of the church's proper mission instead of actually doing the mission.

In the recent past, Lutherans have given a great deal of attention, time, and energy to internal struggles and organizational realignments. A major struggle within The Lutheran Church–Missouri Synod has affected all of America's Lutherans. Lutheran gatherings in recent years have spent large blocks of time discussing the "Missouri Affair." Most Americans cannot distinguish among Lutherans and hence all Lutherans are faced again and again with the task of explaining the struggle in The Lutheran Church–Missouri Synod. The Lutheran mergers of the early 1960s were preceded by years of attention to organizational matters. By the late 1960s both The American Lutheran Church and the Lutheran Church in America found it necessary to undertake additional major organizational restructuring. This again resulted in the churches giving a major priority to organizational concerns.

Now, in the mid 1970s, the reorganizations are complete. The Lutheran Church–Missouri Synod struggle drags on. The various social crises continue to beset both our land and the whole world. The secularizing of society continues unabated. One thing is certain. Lutheran congregations must give a major priority to evangelical outreach no matter what other issues demand our attention.

A Time for Confidence

Lutheran people have lacked confidence in what they have to offer. Lutherans have been intimidated, uncertain whether they have what people need for Christian health and well being. It is not so much that we mistrust God as that we mistrust our ability to be a strong church with a strong witness. When it comes to giving direct personal witness to Christ and his church, we find our courage lacking. Where do we start? How far can we legitimately infringe on the privacy of others? What if we sound like fools? What if the response is a question we cannot answer? Will an attempt to speak to Christ sour our friendship with others? Will we be considered religious fanatics?

Such doubts and fears play into that peculiar

A Time to Reach Out

element of shame that is present in many of us when we would speak of our most deeply held convictions. It is to that the Apostle Paul wrote in his letter to the Romans, "I am not ashamed of the gospel: it is the power of God for salvation to everyone who has faith." Instead of shame, our faith gives us confidence. What if somebody does think us fools? Was it not the same for Christ himself? Did not the Apostle Paul discover the freedom that comes when one is willing to be "a fool for Christ's sake"? What if we are self-conscious and ill at ease in our initial attempts at speaking the good word from God? Does not the maturing process require us to overcome many such hurdles? When it comes right down to it, who are the fools?

God has given us reason to have confidence in him. He is the one who makes something of our evangelical outreach. Through the Holy Spirit he is able to take our witness and use it to convince and persuade others. He is the one who calls us to cut through fear, doubt, and shame, and speak openly of the hope we have in Christ. The gospel is the power of God for salvation. That ought to be enough to stiffen our backbone for witness.

It is not that Christians have ready answers for all human problems. It is not that we count ourselves clever or of superior intellect. It is not that we can present lives that are unsullied by sin.

It is not that congregations of Christians are always attractive. God has staked out his claim on our hearts. That is what gives us the courage to bear witness to him. God's Spirit has called us through the gospel and he will do the same with others. We can trust him. We can go out with confidence that the gospel is the power of God. When that burns itself into our hearts and minds, we are ready to share in the church's evangelical outreach.

The witness of people of faith is always most impressive and attractive precisely in times of uncertainty. It is the ability to stand firm in the throes of battle that testifies to the strength of faith's conviction. It is through witness in the midst of uncertainty and even danger that we learn how to witness in all circumstances. Read through the Acts of the Apostles again. The Apostles knew enough about life's uncertainties and ambiguities. They had nothing easier than we and many things more difficult. They faced the difficulties, struggled with them, prayed over them, and just kept on preaching the message that in Christ is salvation for all. Now it is our turn. There is no reason to wait for a better day.

A Time to Repent

The results of a failure to be zealous in evangelical outreach are apparent. Church attendance

A Time to Reach Out

slacks off. Church membership dwindles. Complaints multiply and a fault-finding develops in congregations. Confidence wanes and it becomes increasingly difficult to invite others to share life in the church.

Lack of vision may cause lack of zeal. Congregations may not see opportunities for outreach in their communities because members look only for people like themselves. Members may err by assuming that certain people, because of different ethnic, cultural, or economic backgrounds or circumstances, would not be open to their invitation. Age, marital status, race, financial well-being— all may be barriers to a vision of the Gospel for all people.

Furthermore, and perhaps as a consequence of a lack of vision and zeal, many congregations are experiencing a heavy rate of "dropouts." This does not refer to those who leave to join other churches. There is always a good deal of movement back and forth among the churches. The tragedy is those who simply drop out of any church.

There is no way for God's people to take the "dropout" phenomenon lightly. Christians are ministers of the grace of God to each other. We are members together in the body of Christ, and members of one another. As a body hurts when it loses a member, so the body of Christ is hurt when it loses a member. Believing as we do that every person is created for life with God and God's people, on earth and in heaven, it is no small matter when a sister or brother disappears from the family. We are responsible for one another.

Repentance is in order where people have been excluded from outreach or members have dropped out without apparent congregational concern. Repentance means to turn around, to go in the opposite direction. It means to actively seek out the unchurched in our communities. It means active efforts to restore those who have become inactive. That is evangelical outreach.

A Time to Reach Out

Since World War II American churches have experienced two widely different eras. In the immediate post-war era people were flocking into the churches. The mere announcement of adult instruction classes often resulted in numbers of people preparing for baptism. By the mid 1960s, however, the scene was just reversed. The number of adults joining the church diminished drastically. Uncertainty and loss of confidence became widespread in the church.

Now a new period is beginning. I believe it is a time made to order for Lutheran strength. There

A Time to Reach Out

is a new openness to the church and its message. People are not seeking out the church, but neither are they turning against it. It is a time when there is a willingness to listen to another's witness. There is a willingness to study and question and consider the Christian message and its implications.

Invitations to share in the church's life and mission are taken seriously. It is a time, therefore, when Christian outreach is essential. It is imperative that God's people invite others to share the faith. There must be unashamed witness to the love of God in Christ. It is a time for people with hearts strong for evangelical outreach.

Lutheran Evangelical Outreach

There is no one "Lutheran" system of evangelical outreach. There are Lutheran congregations with a long history of participation in mass evangelism. Other congregations have highly organized programs of evangelism visitation. Most Lutheran evangelical outreach has depended on the invitation of individual members. It has resulted from natural interpersonal relationships. The witness has been low-key, non-spectacular and has shunned any highly emotional approach. Emphasis has been on the long, steady pull of discipleship rather than on making a decision for Christ now. Instruction in the faith has played an important part in preparation for baptism or adult affirmation of faith. Lutheran evangelical outreach at its best, whatever its methods, has been and should be confessional, congregational, and catechetical.

Confessional Evangelical Outreach

Lutherans have a distinctive doctrine and practice that will speak to great numbers of Americans who are outside the church. The distinctively Lutheran characteristics are sturdy and steady in the face of many winds of opinion about God and people. That is not to say there is a special Lutheran Gospel. It is to say that Lutherans have grasped the central biblical themes, embodied them in confessional statements, and insisted that the church's teaching and practice be consistent with those confessions. It is to say that human moods and fancies change from day to day, but that the Gospel message does not change. The confessions assure the consistency of Christian witness from generation to generation.

At the heart of Lutheran witness is the confession that sinful human beings are justified by God's grace through faith in Jesus Christ. The focus is always on God, on God's grace, and not on people's actions. The focus is on Christ, his life, crucifixion, and resurrection, not on humanity's successes and failures. The focus is on trusting Jesus, not on trusting one's own faith.

The grace of God is the basic biblical theme that informs the central doctrinal affirmations of Lutheran churches. The church itself is understood as a creation of God's grace, a people called together by the Spirit of God through the Gospel. The church is not the result of like-minded people's decision to form a new club, but is the result of God's calling together a people who will follow Christ. The sacraments of the church are God's selected means for sharing himself with his people, not rituals devised by people in order to satisfy their human needs.

Lutheran evangelical outreach, therefore, concentrates on declaring the word of God. The confessions of the church require it. God has given his church a story to tell, a story that describes his gracious love for a sinful humanity. It is in the telling of the story of Jesus Christ that the Spirit of God reaches into human hearts and creates faith in him. It is in declaring God's promise of eternal life through Christ that eternal life becomes a present reality for people who hear.

Confessional evangelical outreach protects the church from shaping the message to please the hearers. It is tempting to provide a message that will assure popularity, a message that will change depending on what people wish to hear. That is not the task our Lord has given his people, however. He commands confessional consistency and clarity in telling the Gospel story. The church can depend on his promise that the word will not return void when the Gospel story is faithfully told.

Confessional evangelical outreach means there will be continuity and consistency in the message of the church. It means that the central content of the Christian faith will be given the central position in the church's witness. It means that our witness to God's saving work through Christ will be descriptive of God's actions. It means that the church's witness will be a faithful witness, faithful to the word given by God himself.

Congregational Evangelical Outreach

Americans have tended to idolize rugged individualism. One of the results of this has been a tendency for people to claim Christian faith and yet treat congregational membership as something to be taken or left, as one wishes. If a person does not like the people in a congregation—leave it. If one is not stirred by the worship and work of a congregation—drop it. Life with God is assumed to be a private matter with congregational participation optional.

In such a private religious world Christian faith becomes a strictly personal matter, a matter between God and each individual. Evangelical outreach can be accomplished by individuals unrelated to congregations and with no significant effort to draw the persons reached into congregations. As a result there have been "no-church" movements in the United States. New denominations have appeared frequently as individuals have found some fault with existing churches and have started a church of their own. Rampant religious individualism makes it necessary to ask whether it is Christ who is authoritative or each individual. Even within existing congregations many members maintain a very marginal relationship with the congregation. Apparently they do not see congregational membership as essential to Christian faith.

Lutheran evangelical outreach is always congregational. The invitation to membership in the body of Christ is always also an invitation to be a member of a congregation. God does not call people to life with himself only. When a person is baptized into Christ he or she is also baptized into the church. Life with God always means life with God's people. Belonging to the church is not optional for those claimed by faith in Christ. Look at the illustrations the Bible uses to describe life with God. Note how all of them describe believers as being bound together with each other as well as with God. In baptism you become a member of God's family, one of his many children. You are one of many citizens in

Lutheran Evangelical Outreach 107

God's kingdom. You are a member of the body of Christ, and individually members of one another. You are one of the sheep in the Good Shepherd's flock. You are one of many building stones built upon the cornerstone, which is Christ. You are one of many branches attached to the vine. God has not made us only to love and serve him. He has also made us to love and serve each other.

The congregation is the primary expression of the church. It is in and through local congregations that the Word of God is preached and the sacraments administered. It is in that local fellowship that we gather around God, present in Word preached and sacrament administered, to worship him with prayer, praise, and thanksgiving. It is in that local congregation that God's people encourage one another, build each other up, bear one another's burdens, minister to each other's needs, and carry on the mission of the church. Christian faith always means participation in a worshiping, witnessing, learning, serving fellowship of believers.

There should be no distinction between lay and clergy as far as responsibility for evangelical outreach is concerned. Lutherans have frequently erred by leaving evangelism to the pastor only. Evangelism is the pastor's responsibility all right, but it is equally the responsibility of all members of the congregation. A congregation cannot be vital unless lay people fulfill their responsibility for evangelical outreach. When both pastors and laity find meaningful ways to participate in reaching out to others the congregation will be lively indeed. Potential for such life exists in every congregation.

Catechetical Evangelical Outreach

Lutherans have always placed strong emphasis on instruction in the Christian faith. Millions of young people have attended years of church school and confirmation instruction as preparation for adult life in the church. Millions of adults have received doctrinal instruction prior to baptism or adult confirmation of faith.

God does not mean for his people to be vague in their understanding of him. Neither does he appeal to us only through inner emotional feelings. He has very explicitly revealed himself to us in the person of Jesus Christ. He expects us to use our heads as well as our feelings in responding to him. It is the church's responsibility to keep the biblical portrayal of Jesus before his people in such a way that both the intelligence and the emotions are stirred. It is also the church's responsibility to help its members understand and appropriate the whole counsel of God found in the Scriptures. That can only be done by continuing instruction in the faith. Such instruction, along with life's experiences, makes possible a continual growth and maturing of Christian faith and life.

Lutheran evangelical outreach presumes the necessity of a catechetical ministry. Biblical teaching and learning must continue if a Christian life is to grow and be healthy. Some teaching and learning is done informally in conversations among friends. Some comes through the regular preaching ministry in a congregation. Some comes through individual or group Bible study. It is important that there also be a disciplined series of classes in which a basic catechism of the Christian faith is explained and studied. Such formal instruction will provide a comprehensive view of the Christian faith. Without it a person's understanding is likely to be fragmentary and remain at an elementary level. Such classes provide an important opportunity for catechumens to ask questions that may trouble them. Class discussions become wide ranging and exciting experiences.

Such organized, comprehensive instruction is catechetical. It may use Luther's Small Catechism or some other summary statement of the Christian faith. It is normally taught by a pastor, but competent lay instruction is just as useful.

Evangelical outreach efforts are most effective

if a member of the congregation invites a nonmember to attend instruction classes with him or her. It is a friendly action. It may help a person move into a new world. At the very least it testifies to a high level of concern. Furthermore, there will almost certainly be after-class questions and discussion. Some of the best opportunities for personal witness occur in those moments. Participation in such instruction classes may prove to be among life's rich experiences for both the member and non-member.

Everybody Participating

Lutheran evangelical outreach has one additional goal. Everybody is asked to participate. That does not mean that everybody should be doing the same thing. Everybody does not have identical capabilities. It is possible, however, for every member to be vitally engaged in a congregation's evangelical outreach.

President Robert Marshall of the Lutheran Church in America has suggested three distinct, important ways to participate in evangelical outreach. The first is *prayer* outreach. Every person is able to be a full participant in this. The intercessory prayers of every member of the congregation are needed. Evangelical outreach efforts will be strong when the prayer efforts are strong.

Lutheran Evangelical Outreach 111

The incapacitated, the shut-in, the isolated person can be the backbone of a congregation's prayer effort. People do not need to be mobile in order to provide undergirding prayer support for a congregation's evangelical outreach.

The second is *friendship* outreach. Again, anybody who can participate in congregational worship can invite friends to accompany them to church. The great majority of adults joining Lutheran churches indicate they were invited to participate by acquaintances from the congregation. Invitations do not need to be limited to worship. People can ask others to join them at Bible studies, adult instruction classes, church school, women's groups, youth groups, musical groups, and any other congregational activities. Such invitations have been the avenues to Christian faith and life for many people. They are almost always grounded in good, old-fashioned neighborliness. Concern for one's neighbors provides many natural opportunities to share the Christian faith. A friend's invitation to take part in the congregation's faith, fellowship, and service is a powerful witness.

The third is *witness* outreach. This involves actually telling the Gospel story. It calls for people who will tell what God has done and is doing. Witness outreach requires pastors and theologically trained people. It requires excellent, articulate lay theologians. It also requires men, women, and children who will testify to the love of Christ at whatever level they know it. A verse in the moving Appalachian folk song "There Is a Balm in Gilead" puts it well:

> *If you cannot preach like Peter;*
> *If you cannot pray like Paul;*
> *You can tell the love of Jesus,*
> *And how he died for all.*

Christian people are called to tirelessly tell the Gospel story. It is the church's duty and joy to sing and shout and say the good news about God's love. When a congregation uses all avenues of outreach—prayer, friendship, and witness—people will be reached. That is what evangelical outreach intends to do.